The “Private” in Private International Law

The "Private" in Private International Law

Symeon C. Symeonides

eleven
international publishing

Published, sold and distributed by Eleven International Publishing
P.O. Box 85576
2508 CG The Hague
The Netherlands
Tel.: +31 70 33 070 33
Fax: +31 70 33 070 30
email: sales@elevenpub.nl
www.elevenpub.com

Sold and distributed in USA and Canada
Independent Publishers Group
814 N. Franklin Street
Chicago, IL 60610, USA
Order Placement: +1 800 888 4741
Fax: +1 312 337 5985
orders@ipgbook.com
www.ipgbook.com

Eleven International Publishing is an imprint of Boom uitgevers Den Haag.

ISBN 978-94-6236-949-8
ISBN 978-94 6274-520-9 (e-book)

Table of Contents

Introduction

When I received this kind invitation to deliver the 'Private Law Lecture' at Maastricht University, I inferred that the inviters assumed that Private International Law (PIL)—the only subject for which I could claim some expertise—is in fact part of private law.[1] In this essay, which is based on that lecture, I do not dispute this assumption, but I hope it would not be impolite if I seek to clarify and qualify it in some significant respects.

The adjective "private" in PIL serves two functions – one external, one internal. Externally, it distinguishes PIL from its public international sibling. Internally, it circumscribes the domestic scope of PIL to horizontal relations, or disputes, between parties other than a state acting in the exercise of governmental authority. In this sense, PIL is unquestionably part of private law. However, when continental writers speak of the 'privateness' of PIL, they tend to assume that PIL disputes implicate *only* the interests of the parties and *not* the interests of their respective home states or the states that have pertinent connections with the dispute. This essay challenges this assumption.

I The Privateness of PIL

A The Continental View

Like much of everything else in classical PIL doctrine, the insistence on the privateness of PIL dates back to the founder of PIL, Friedrich Carl von Savigny.[2] Like most nineteenth century writers, Savigny sharply distinguished private from public law and placed PIL exclusively and firmly in the private-law side of the divide. In his view, public law was political while private law was pure and apolitical, emanating directly from the people's spirit (*Volksgeist*) untainted by political motives. Specifically, Savigny postulated that PIL consisted, or should consist, of neutral, evenhanded, bilateral choice-of-law rules that:

1 Indeed, the teaching of PIL at the Maastricht University Law School is the responsibility of the Private Law Department rather than, for example, the Department of International and European Law.

2 *See* F.C. von Savigny, *System des heutigen römischen Rechts*, at 2 (1849), English translation by William Guthrie, under the title *Private International Law, A Treatise on the Conflict of Laws and the Limits of their Operation in Respect of Place and Time* (1869). Hereinafter, all references to Savigny are to this translation, abbreviated as Savigny, *Treatise*. Of course, the distinction between public and private law preceded Savigny by at least sixteen centuries, dating back to Ulpian. *See Corpus Juris Civilis* 1.1. §2 ("*Huius studii duae sunt positiones, publicum et privatum. Publicum ius est quod ad statum rei romanae spectat; privatum quod ad singulorum utilitatem. Sunt enim quaedam publice utilia, quaedam privatim.*").

1. Place foreign law and litigants on parity with forum law and litigants,
2. Assign each legal relation to one particular state, regardless of that state's actual or imputed "wish" to apply its law and regardless of that law's content, and
3. Aspire to produce international decisional harmony, regardless of which state's courts adjudicate the case.[3]

Savigny recognized that the equal treatment of forum and foreign law, as well as domestic and foreign litigants, would be impeded if the forum state could freely invoke its own interests. This is why, although he praised Joseph Story's "excellent work"[4] and drew several elements from it, Savigny rejected Story's characterization of PIL as a "branch of public law."[5] Indeed, Story, who in his 1834 *Commentaries* was the first writer to use the term "private international law" for what was known, since Huber's time, as the law of conflict of laws,[6] wrote that:

> The jurisprudence … arising from the conflict of the laws of different nations … is a most interesting and important branch of public law.… This branch of public law may be fitly denominated private international law, since it is chiefly seen and felt in its application to the common business of private persons, and rarely rises to the dignity of national negotiations, or national controversies.[7]

The use of both adjectives (public and private) in the above excerpt is not a contradiction. They simply refer to the operation of PIL in the international and domestic arenas, respectively. In the international realm, PIL is private (as opposed to public international law), in that it deals with "the common business of private persons" rather than "national controversies,"[8] *i.e.*, disputes between states as such. However, in the domestic arena, PIL is a "branch of public law" because the fundamental question in conflicts cases is whether

3 For documentation and discussion, see S.C. Symeonides, "Private International Law: Idealism, Pragmatism, Eclecticism", 384 *Recueil des cours*, 48-53, *et passim* (2017) (copyright by The Hague Academy of International Law) [hereinafter Symeonides, *Idealism*]. This essay draws heavily from this publication.

4 *See* Savigny, *Treatise*, at p. 2 (referring to "the excellent work of Story, which is also extremely useful, as a rich collection of materials, for every inquirer.").

5 J. Story, *Commentaries on the Conflict of Laws*, at § 9 (1834).

6 *See* U. Huber, "De conflictu legum diversarum in diversis imperiis," in U. Huber, *Praelectiones Juris Romani et Hodierni* (1689). The name private international law began gaining wider acceptance in Europe after a German book and then a French book, published seven and nine years, respectively, after Story's book, used *internationalen Privatrechts* and *droit international privé* in their titles. *See* W. Schaeffner, *Entwicklung des internationalen Privatrechts* (1841); G. Foelix, *Droit international privé ou du conflit des lois de différentes nations en matière de droit privé* (1843).

7 Story, *Commentaries*, at § 9.

8 *Id.*

to apply foreign law, and the answer to that question depends on "comity," which is the "express or tacit consent" of a *state.*[9]

Obviously, Story's central focus on states as the principal PIL actors was inimical if not completely antithetical to Savigny's vision of international uniformity, which presupposed that states would act unselfishly,[10] as well as the concomitant principle of equal treatment of forum and foreign law and litigants, a principle from which Savigny allowed only two narrow exceptions. The first was the *ordre public* exception.[11] The second referred to foreign laws "of a strictly positive, imperative nature, which are consequently inconsistent with that freedom of application which pays no regard to the limits of particular states."[12] This was the first recognition of what later became known as 'overriding mandatory rules.' However, Savigny viewed these rules as highly exceptional and clearly did not anticipate their subsequent increasing recognition or proliferation. To the contrary, he characterized these rules as "anomalous"[13] and expressed the belief that they would disappear over time. Savigny stated that, in cases falling within these exceptions, the judge "will have to apply the domestic law more exclusively than that the principle [of equal treatment] allows, and must, on the other hand, leave the foreign law unapplied, even where that principle would justify its application."[14]

More than a century later, another great German author, Gerhard Kegel, articulated in more explicit terms the privateness of PIL. Distinguishing between public and private law, Kegel declared that "the state has no interest in the field of private law in applying its own law to the maximum exclusion of foreign law";[15] and, conversely, "the state does not suffer, it is not hurt, if in some cases … foreign law is applied."[16] In dealing with conflicts cases, the state "is playing the role of the judge, not of litigant…. It does not decide its own affairs but the affairs of *others,*"[17] even if one or both parties are the state's own citizens. As another European writer recently noted:

---

9 *See id.* at § 23 ("[W]hatever force and obligation the laws of one country have in another, depend solely upon the laws, and municipal regulations of the latter, that is to say, upon its own proper jurisprudence and polity, and upon its own express or tacit consent.").

10 *See* Savigny, *Treatise,* at 92-93 (noting that, in enacting a particular rule, national legislatures should "always … ask [themselves] whether such a rule would be well adapted for reception into that common statute law of all nations.").

11 *See id.* at 34 (noting that "[l]egal institutions of a foreign state, of which the existence is not at all recognised in ours, and which, therefore, have no claim to the protection of our courts.").

12 *Id.*

13 *See id.* at 38. Savigny mentioned as examples of such rules the prohibitions against polygamy and acquisition of realty by Jews. *See id.* at 36.

14 *Id.* at 34.

15 G. Kegel, "The Crisis of Conflict of Laws," 112 *Recueil des cours* 91, 184 (1964).

16 *Id.* at 182-83.

17 *Id.* at 182.

> [P]rivate law—unlike public law—is neutral and apolitical. It does not incorporate state interests and has no socially constitutive functions. Instead, it orders personal activities and freedoms and regulates interests of private parties. Cases with ties to multiple legal orders are, therefore, not a matter of conflicts between states and state interests but clashes between private intentions and individual spheres of freedom.[18]

Today, the public-private law division is deeply ingrained in continental legal thinking. For evidence to that effect, one need not look farther than this host institution, the Law School of Maastricht University, which has separate Private Law and Public Law departments.

B American Perspectives

American law schools are not organized by departments, but, even if they were, it is highly unlikely that they would establish them along the private-public law divide. Indeed, throughout its short history, American law never fully accepted this divide. At most, it tolerated it and sometimes used it restrictively. Joseph Story subscribed to the private-public distinction,[19] perhaps because, unlike most of his contemporaries, he was exceptionally familiar with continental literature.[20] However, as noted earlier, he classified PIL as a "branch of public law."[21] In domestic law, the distinction gained some traction later in the nineteenth century, fueled by a political movement to protect contract and property rights from "the dangerous and unstable redistributive tendencies of democratic politics."[22]

However, with the turn of the twentieth century and the Supreme Court's 1905 decision in *Lochner v. New York*,[23] which constitutionalized freedom of contract, this distinction began to encounter opposition. The opposition then became a full-scale attack under the banner of the American Legal Realist Movement of the 1920s and 1930s. This movement challenged the basic premise behind any assumption that private law could be neutral and apolitical, arguing that the use of state coercion to enforce rules of contract and property

18 G. Rühl, "Unilateralism," in J. Basedow, K. Hopt & R. Zimmermann (eds.), *Max Planck Encyclopedia of European Private Law* (2012).
19 *See* Justice Story's concurring opinion in *Trustees of Dartmouth College v. Woodward*, 17 U.S. (4 Wheat.) 518, 559, 669-73 (1819).
20 *See* S.C. Symeonides, *Oxford Commentaries on American Law: Choice of Law*, 46 (2016).
21 Story, *Commentaries*, at § 9 (quoted *supra*).
22 *See* M.J. Horwitz, "The History of the Public/Private Distinction," 130 *U. Pa. L. Rev.* 1423, 1425 (1982).
23 198 U.S. 45 (1905).

law meant that those rules represented the exercise of public power as much as the rules of antitrust law.[24] "By 1940, it was a sign of legal sophistication to understand the arbitrariness of the division of law into public and private realms."[25] PIL scholars of that period, such as Walter W. Cook and later Brainerd Currie who later led the American choice-of-law revolution, took those views for granted in formulating their choice-of-law approaches.[26]

Since then, American writers have repeatedly voiced their "doubts as to the substance, and indeed the supposed naturality of the distinction between the public and private legal spheres."[27] In the 1990s, Critical Legal Studies scholars[28] "made the debunking of the public/private divide a centerpiece of much of their thinking and a cornerstone in their argument, if not for a strong state, then at least for a treatment of (apolitical) 'private' law as (political) public law."[29] More recently, one author wrote that "[a]ll law is public,"[30] and thus the term private law is "an oxymoron."[31] This view comes with PIL implications:

> If there is no private law, there can be no private international law.... The central issue in ... private international law ... is a fundamental issue of state authority; namely, which state will be allocated the legal power to regulate the matter? The proposition that all law is public indicates that all conflict of laws issues are issues of allocation of public power.[32]

To be sure, even if one accepts the view that "all law is public," one can still differentiate between various gradations, or categories, of "public" laws. For example, American courts do not apply foreign criminal laws, tax laws, or antitrust laws[33] but do apply other foreign laws, such as tort and contract laws.[34] The focus of our inquiry is on how PIL systems

24 *See, e.g.*, M.R. Cohen, "The Basis of Contract," 46 *Harv. L. Rev.* 553 (1933); M.R. Cohen, "Property and Sovereignty," 13 *Cornell L. Q.* 8 (1927); L.L. Fuller & W.R. Perdue, "The Reliance Interest in Contract Damages," 46 *Yale L.J.* 52 (1936); R.L. Hale, "Force and the State: A Comparison of 'Political' and 'Economic' Compulsion," 35 *Colum. L. Rev.* 149 (1935).

25 M.J. Horwitz, "The History of the Public/Private Distinction," 130 *U. Pa. L. Rev.* 1423, 1427 (1982).

26 *See* W.W. Cook, "The Logical and Legal Bases of the Conflict of Laws," 33 *Yale L.J.* 457 (1924).

27 H. Muir Watt (ed.), *Private International Law and Public Law* xiv (vol. 1, 2015).

28 *See, e.g.*, D. Kennedy, "The Stages of the Decline of the Public/Private Distinction," 130 *U. Pa. L. Rev.* 1349 (1982); M. Horwitz, *supra.*

29 R. Michaels & N. Jansen, "Private Law beyond the State? Europeanization, Globalization, Privatization," 54 *Am. J. Comp. L.* 843, 857 (2006).

30 J.P. Trachtman, "The International Economic Law Revolution," 17 *J. Int'l L.* 33, 40 (1996).

31 *Id.* at 34.

32 *Id.* at 40.

33 *See* S.C. Symeonides, *Oxford Commentaries on American Law: Choice of Law*, 82-86 (2016).

34 Moreover, the method used by the Supreme Court in defining the extraterritorial reach of certain federal statutes such as the Sherman (antitrust) Act differs from the method used in resolving ordinary tort or contract conflicts. *See* W.S. Dodge, "The Public-Private Distinction in the Conflict of Laws," 18 *Duke J. Comp. & Int'l L.* 371, 372 (2008):

handle conflicts involving those "other" laws. On the other hand, even if one completely rejects the view that "all law is public," one can still question Kegel's statement that, in conflicts cases, the state acts as a neutral "judge" of "the affairs of others." Indeed, although that statement continues to reflect the classic PIL doctrine, more recent statements by other German writers suggest that this view is no longer universally accepted. For example, Erik Jayme writes that "what really characterizes contemporary PIL is a conflict of cultures,"[35] and Karl Kreuzer uses the hyperbolic phrase "clash of civilizations."[36] The term "conflict of laws," by which this subject is known in the United States, is far less dramatic, but: (1) it signifies the inherent difference between domestic cases, which implicate the values of only one state, and multistate cases, which involve the laws of more than one state, which often embody different objectives, policies, or values; and (2) it recognizes that a state has as much of a reason to be concerned with the latter cases as with the former.

This difference partially explains, but does not necessarily justify, Brainerd Currie's view that the forum state cannot—indeed *should not*—profess impartiality in any clash involving its own values. The next section examines this position (which is diametrically opposed to Savigny's private, apolitical view of PIL), as well as the in-between possibilities.

C The Outlier: Brainerd Currie and State Interests

For Savigny, most private law is apolitical; for Currie, all law must be understood as political."[37] This statement may be hyperbolic,[38] but it provides a starting point for a

In a torts case, the court looks to the particular forum's choice-of-law rules to determine which jurisdiction's substantive law should apply. If the answer is foreign law, the court applies that law and decides the case on the merits. In an antitrust case, by contrast, the court does not look to the forum's choice-of-law rules to decide which antitrust law should govern. Instead, it construes its own antitrust law to decide whether that law reaches the case, and if it does not, the court simply dismisses the claim. Under no circumstances does the court decide the case by applying foreign antitrust law.

35 E. Jayme, "Identité culturelle et intégration: Le droit international privé postmoderne," 251 *Recueil des cours* 9, 52 (1995) ("En fait, ce qui vraiment caractérise le droit international privé actuel, ce sont les conflits de cultures.").

36 K. Kreuzer, "Clash of Civilizations and Conflict of Laws," 62 *Rev. hellénique dr. int'l* 629 (2009).

37 R. Michaels, "Post-critical Private International Law: From Politics to Technique," in H. Muir Watt & D.P. Fernández Arroyo (eds.), *Private International Law and Global Governance* 54, 62 (2014).

38 In fact, Michaels sees a "remarkable similarity" between Currie and Savigny:

On the one hand, Savigny agrees with Currie that politically relevant laws of the forum trump any colliding claims for application from foreign law. On the other hand, Currie agrees with Savigny that cases that do not involve policy interests of states—"no interest cases"—cannot be resolved with his method. Where they differ is the degree to which laws without policies exist. Whereas Savigny considers substantive interests and policies in private law largely irrelevant ..., they are central to Currie's analysis.

Michaels, *supra* previous note, at 62-63. Further, Michaels correctly notes that "Currie is actually more open to the application of foreign laws: whereas Savigny does not envisage the applicability of foreign political laws at all, Currie favors it in cases where the forum is uninterested." *Id.* at 62 n. 33.

comparison. Currie's notion that states have an interest in the resolution of multistate disputes between private parties was simply the natural extension of his legal realist view of law as "an instrument of social control," and his "emphasis on the economic and social policies expressed in laws."[39] Currie postulated that, whenever a case falls within a law's spatial reach as delineated by the interpretative process, the state from which that law emanates has a "governmental interest" in its application in order to effectuate the policy embodied in that law. In Currie's words, an "interest ... is the product of (1) a governmental policy and (2) the concurrent existence of an appropriate relationship between the state having the policy and the transaction, the parties, or the litigation."[40]

The concept of state interests in this context was not a novelty in American law.[41] In fact, Fritz Juenger claims that Currie "was original only in the sense that he reinvented the wheel."[42] In any event, the idea that states have an interest in applying their law to disputes between private parties had appeared prominently in a cluster of U.S. Supreme Court decisions issued in the 1930's interpreting the Full Faith and Credit clause of the Constitution.[43] What was new was Currie's partisan articulation of state interests. Besides the inaccuracy of the adjective "governmental" (as opposed to "state" or "public" interests),

---

39 B. Currie, *Selected Essays on the Conflict of Laws*, 64 (1963) [hereinafter Currie, *Selected Essays*] ("Law is an instrument of social control. Recognition of this fact, and emphasis on the economic and social policies expressed in laws, would lead to a fresh and constructive approach to conflict-of-laws problems."). For a discussion of the influence of American legal realism on American conflicts law, *see* S. Symeonides, *An Outsider's View of the American Approach to Choice of Law: Comparative Observations on Current American and Continental Conflicts Doctrine* 214-21 (1980); C.W. Fassberg, "Realism and Revolution in Conflict of Laws: In with a Bang and Out with a Whimper," 163 *U. Pa. L. Rev.* 1919 (2015).

40 Currie, *Selected Essays,* 621.

41 In fact, one could argue that the same was true of European law, or at least European legal literature. For similar ideas in European literature, *see, e.g.,* A. Flessner, *Interessenjurisprudenz im Internationalen Privatrecht* (1990); C. Joerges, *Zum Funktionswandel des Kollisionsrechts* (1971); R. Quadri, *Lezioni de diritto internazionale privato* (3rd ed. 1961); A. Heini, "Neuere Strömungen im amerikanischen internationalen Privatrecht," 19 *Schweizerisches Jahrbuch für Internationales Recht* 31 (1962); C. Joerges, "Vorüberlegungen zu einer Theorie des internationalen Wirtschaftsrechts," 43 *RabelsZ* 6 (1979); H. Kronstein, "Crisis of 'Conflict of Laws,'" 37 *Geo. L. J.* 483 (1948-49); R. Wiethölter, "Vorbemerkungen zum IPR," in Deutscher Rat für IPR Erbrechtskommission, *Internationales Nachlaßverfahrensrecht, Vorschläge und Gutachten zur Reform des deutschen internationalen Erbrechts,* 142 (1969); R. Wiethölter, "Begriffs- und Interessenjurisprudenz -falsche Fronten im IPR," in G. Kegel, H-J. Musielak & K. Schurig, *Festschrift für Kegel,* 213, 224, 233, 239, 260 (1977).

42 F.K. Juenger, "American and European Conflicts Law," 30 *Am. J. Comp. L.* 117, 119 (1982). Juenger continues as follows:

If [Currie] had read Beale's translation of Bartolus he would have appreciated the venerable age of the idea that choice-of-law problems can be resolved by the 'ordinary processes of construction and interpretation' ... [and] that the attempt to divine the spatial reach of rules from their underlying policies is several.

Id.

43 *See Bradford Elec. Light Co. v. Clapper,* 286 U.S. 145 (1932); *Alaska Packers Ass'n v. Indus. Accident Comm'n,* 294 U.S. 532 (1935); *Pacific Employers Ins. Co. v. Indus. Accident Comm'n,* 306 U.S. 493 (1939). *See also Watson v. Employers Liab. Assur. Corp. Ltd.,* 348 U.S. 66 (1954).

which provided an easy target for critics, Currie's articulation of state interests suffers from several serious flaws. In particular:

1. It was "imperialistic" in essentially ascribing to the state a selfish wish to maximize its gains at the expense of the policies of other states, as opposed to avoiding impairment of its own strongly held policies and values;[44]
2. It was partisan in postulating that, in the vast majority of cases, a state has an interest in applying its law only when it would benefit its domiciliaries, but not when it would benefit similarly situated non-domiciliaries[45] (a notion referred to hereafter as Currie's "personal-law principle"); and
3. It was narrow in at least two respects:
   a. In failing to consider a state's "multistate" interests—namely, interests that stem from the state's membership in a broader community of states, but are not reflected directly in a state's domestic law;[46] and
   b. In disregarding the interests of the individual litigants, under the dubious reasoning that those interests are always "subsumed" into the interests of each litigant's home state.[47]

Given these shortcomings, one would be justified in asking why the concept of state interests is even discussed here. It is because, at its core, state interest is a valid concept, even if Currie articulated it in extreme terms. Indeed, contemporary states have certain interests in the outcome of multistate disputes between private parties. The relevant question is not whether such interests exist, but rather whether a recognition of their existence facilitates or impedes a rational resolution of conflicts of laws.

---

44 *See infra* II.C.

45 Currie argued that a state has an interest in applying its pro-plaintiff rules only for the benefit of local plaintiffs and its pro-defendant rules only for the benefit of local defendants. *See* Currie, *Selected Essays*, 691–721 (arguing that New York's unlimited compensatory damages law "is not for the protection of all who buy tickets in New York, or board planes there. It is for the protection of New York people."). *See also* Currie, *Selected Essays*, 724, 785–86 (arguing that a state that has a guest statute or a pro-defendant contract rule has an interest in applying them only if the defendants are domiciled in that state).

46 Currie specifically dismissed the view that a state should be guided in its choice-of-law decisions by the "needs of the interstate and international system." Currie, *Selected Essays*, 614. He asserted that the traditional system, because of its international origins, was overtaken by "the compulsion of internationalist and altruist ideals" and had "guiltily suppressed the natural instincts of community self-interest … [and] enforce[d] a purposeless self-denial." *Id.* at 525. In order to compensate, Currie championed "the rational, moderate and controlled pursuit of self-interest." *Id.* These adjectives offered some reassurance, as did Currie's statements that "[t]he shortsighted, selfish state is nothing more than an experimental model," and "[n]o such state exists, at least in this country." *Id.* at 616. Nevertheless, both the tenor and many of the specifics of his theory were far less moderate.

47 *See* Currie, *Selected Essays*, 610 (Currie found "no place in conflict-of-laws analysis for a calculus of private interests [because] [b]y the time the interstate plane is reached the resolution of conflicting private interests has been achieved; it is subsumed in the statement of the laws of the respective states.").

II PIL and State Interests

A *Do States Have an Interest in Multistate Disputes between Private Parties?*

Currie's approach encountered widespread criticism in the United States and abroad, both of which are discussed in detail elsewhere.[48] The following discussion is limited to one key element of Currie's approach, the central concept of state interests. It begins with the basic question of whether states have an interest in the outcome of multistate disputes between private parties, a question that all of Currie's critics answer in the negative. One of the most caustic critics, Friedrich Juenger, argued that the notion of a state interest in this context is "a highly implausible construct"[49] and rejected Currie's "hypothesis" that states have "a deep-seated concern in the implementation of their legal rules."[50] Juenger criticized Currie and his followers for "[not] adducing empirical evidence for this hypothesis."[51] Similarly, a later critic asked rhetorically, "Can anyone cite a case in which a state appeared as amicus curiae arguing the importance that its own law be applied?"[52] If it were true that "[s]tates often appear as amicus curiae asserting interests they do hold dear,"[53] the argument goes, states would submit amicus curiae briefs urging a court to apply their respective laws. Do they?

In the United States, the answer is yes. There is a plethora of empirical evidence on both the existence and the assertion of state interests in the outcome of choice-of-law disputes. For example, in practically every major international maritime conflicts case that has reached the U.S. Supreme Court, at least one foreign government, and occasionally the U.S. government, has filed amicus curiae briefs bringing to the Court's attention their interests in the outcome of litigation between ship owners and seamen.[54] The same is true of most other international conflicts that come before the U.S. Supreme Court. In *Hartford Fire Ins. Co. v. California,*[55] the British government submitted an amicus brief urging the

48 For multiple references and discussion, *see* S.C. Symeonides, *The American Choice-of-Law Revolution: Past, Present, and Future,* 22-24, *et passim* (2006). For discussion of Currie's approach, *see id.* 13-24, 365-84, *et passim.*

49 F.K. Juenger, *Choice of Law and Multistate Justice,* 135 (1993).

50 *Id.*

51 *Id.*

52 M.H. Gottesman, "Adrift in the Sea of Indeterminacy," 75 *Ind. L.J.* 527, 531 (2000).

53 *Id.*

54 For references, *see* the authorities cited in S.C. Symeonides, "Maritime Conflicts of Law from the Perspective of Modern Choice of Law Methodology," *Tul. Mar. L. J.* 223, 224-225, 228, 247 (1982).

55 509 U.S. 764 (1993).

application of British law in a dispute involving British reinsurers.[56] Since then, many more foreign governments (including the EU Commission on behalf of the twenty-eight EU states) have filed amici briefs, asserting their respective interests and urging the Court not to apply U.S. law. The following list is illustrative of recent cases wherein such briefs were filed, with the number of foreign government amici briefs indicated in parentheses: *American Insurance Ass'n v. Garamendi*[57] (two); *Sosa v. Alvarez-Machain*[58] (one); *F. Hoffman-La Roche Ltd. v. Empagran S.A.*[59] (ten); *Kiobel v. Royal Dutch Petroleum Co.*[60] (five); *Morrison v. National Australia Bank Ltd.*[61] (three). Additionally, countless amici briefs (in some cases, over a hundred) are filed by American, foreign, and international non-governmental organizations, law professors, and other individuals invoking public interests implicated in disputes between private litigants.

This phenomenon is not confined to international conflicts. For example, in *Clay v. Sun Insurance Office, Ltd.*,[62] an interstate conflict involving an insurance dispute between private parties, the Florida Attorney General appeared before the U.S. Supreme Court to defend Florida's interests in applying its law.[63] In *Bernhard v. Harrah's Club*,[64] in which a California court applied California tort law imposing civil liability on a Nevada casino, the State of Nevada filed an amicus brief supporting the casino's petition for writ of certiorari to the U.S. Supreme Court.

Finally, such briefs are not uncommon in state courts, or in lower federal courts. In *Kearney v. Salomon Smith Barney, Inc.*,[65] a tort dispute between a Georgia brokerage firm and its California clients, the California Attorney General filed an amicus brief in the California court supporting the application of California law. In *Modern Computer Systems v. Modern Banking Systems*,[66] a contract dispute between a Minnesota franchisee and a Nebraska

56 *Id.* at 798 (citing Brief for Government of United Kingdom of Great Britain and Northern Ireland as Amicus Curiae Supporting Petitioners).

57 539 U.S. 396 (2003).

58 542 U.S. 692 (2004).

59 542 U.S. 155 (2004).

60 569 U.S. 108 (2013).

61 561 U.S. 247 (2010).

62 363 U.S. 207 (1960).

63 *Clay* involved the question of whether Florida could constitutionally apply a statute that prohibited a contractual shortening of the limitation period for suing an insurer, on a policy issued in Illinois to an insured who later moved to Florida and sustained loss while there. The U.S. Supreme Court held that Florida could do so, in part because of its interests in protecting insureds who sustain losses within its territory. The Court noted that: "Florida's particular interest in this very statute is shown by the fact that the Attorney General of the State filed briefs and participated in oral arguments to support the … [statute's] constitutionality[.]" 363 U.S. at 216.

64 546 P.2d 719 (Cal. 1976), *cert. denied*, 429 U.S. 859 (1977).

65 137 P.3d 914 (Cal. 2006).

66 858 F.2d 1339 (8th Cir. 1988) (decided under Nebraska conflicts law), *rev'd*, 871 F.2d 734 (8th Cir. 1989).

franchisor, the Minnesota Attorney General appeared as an amicus in a federal district court in Nebraska and argued for the application of Minnesota law.[67] These cases serve as a good reminder that disputes between private parties may implicate not only the interests of the parties, but also those of their respective states.

To be sure, amicus briefs are not the only evidence of a state's interest in the application of its law. One can find better evidence by looking at the actual wording of state statutes. Despite statements that statutes "do not come equipped with labels proclaiming their spatial dimension,"[68] or that "legislatures *have* no actual intent on territorial reach,"[69] such evidence is plentiful. It answers the rhetorical question of whether "any state legislature declared it important that its substantive law be chosen in some defined category of cases having multistate contacts?"[70]

In the United States, again the answer is "yes." As I have documented in another publication, several state statutes contain "localizing rules" consisting of precisely such declarations.[71] These rules proclaim that the statutes that contain them (such as statutes regulating consumer, employment, insurance, franchise, distributorship, and agency contracts) shall apply to transactions or events with certain enumerated connections to the enacting state. Some of these rules even expressly prohibit the contractual choice of another state's law. The statutes do not use phrases such as "conflict of laws" or "choice of law," which is why they can easily elude an electronic word search. Even so, they do carry conspicuous "labels proclaiming their spatial dimension."[72] In the awkward, anthropomorphic terminology of interest analysis, these statutes proclaim the enacting state's "interest" (or *volonté d'application)* in regulating the enumerated multistate transactions. Moreover, as also documented in the same publication, localized statutes are by no means an American phenomenon.

B Are State Interests Ascertainable?

It is true, however, that statutes expressly declaring their intended extraterritorial reach are the exception rather than the rule. Most statutes are either silent on the question of

67 For numerous additional examples of state attorneys general appearing on the side of a private litigant and advocating for their respective states' interests, *see* S.C. Symeonides, "American Choice of Law at the Dawn of the Twenty-first Century," 37 *Willamette L. Rev.* 1, 23-24 (2000).

68 F.K. Juenger, "Conflict of Laws: A Critique of Interest Analysis," 32 *Am. J. Comp. L.* 1, 35 (1984).

69 L. Brilmayer, "Interest Analysis and the Myth of Legislative Intent," 78 *Mich. L. Rev.* 392, 393 (1980) (hereinafter Brilmayer, "The Myth").

70 M.H. Gottesman, "Adrift in the Sea of Indeterminacy," 75 *Ind. L.J.* 527, 531 (2000).

71 *See* Symeonides, *Idealism*, 172-79.

72 F.K. Juenger, "Conflict of Laws: A Critique of Interest Analysis," 32 *Am. J. Comp. L.* 1, 35 (1984).

their application to foreign cases, or contain "boilerplate language"[73] whose "literal catholicity,"[74] if taken at face value, would make them applicable to any and all activities, territorial or extraterritorial. As Currie observed, "Lawgivers ... are accustomed to speak[ing] in terms of unqualified generality ... [using] words like 'all,' 'every,' 'no,' 'any,' and 'whoever'"[75] because "they ordinarily give no thought to the phenomena that would suggest the need for qualification."[76] For example, the Jones Act purports to provide a remedy to "[a]ny seaman"[77] who suffers an injury in the course of his employment. Similarly, the Americans with Disabilities Act (ADA) provides that "[n]o individual" shall be discriminated against on the basis of disability by "any person" who owns or operates a place of "public accommodation."[78]

In cases involving such statutes, it falls upon courts to determine which of the "any and all" persons or activities the legislature intended to regulate. Courts discharge this task daily, by determining "whether 'any' or 'every' reaches to the limits of the enacting authority's usual scope or is to be applied to foreign events or transactions."[79] This is what Currie meant when he wrote that the court should resort to the method of statutory "construction and interpretation" that is typically employed in fully domestic cases. In a statement that accidentally echoed Savigny, Currie wrote, "Just as we determine by that process how a statute applies in time, and how it applies to marginal cases, so we may determine how it should be applied to cases involving foreign elements."[80]

Currie's critics charged that his "domestic method" of statutory construction and interpretation failed to recognize the differences between domestic and multistate cases,[81] and was

73 *Hartford Fire Ins. Co. v. California*, 509 U.S. 764, 813 (1993); *EEOC v. Arabian Am. Oil Co.*, 499 U.S. 244, 249 (1991).

74 *Lauritzen v. Larsen*, 345 U.S. 571, 576 (1953).

75 Currie, *Selected Essays*, 81.

76 *Id.* at 82.

77 46 U.S.C. § 688. For cases involving the extraterritorial reach of the Jones Act, *see* S.C. Symeonides, "Maritime Conflicts of Law from the Perspective of Modern Choice of Law Methodology," 7 *Tul. Mar. L. J.* 223 (1982).

78 42 U.S.C. § 12182(a). For the question of whether the ADA applies to foreign cruise ships while in U.S. waters, *see Spector v. Norwegian Cruise Line Ltd*, 545 U.S. 119 (2005) (discussed in S.C. Symeonides, "Cruising in American Waters: Spector, Maritime Conflicts, and Choice of Law," 37 *J. Mar. L. & Com.* 491 (2006)).

79 *Lauritzen*, 345 U.S. at 578-79.

80 Currie, *Selected Essays*, 184. The quoted statement superficially resembles Savigny's analogy between local or territorial limits (*Oertliche Gränzen*) and time limits (*Zeitliche Gränzen*) in the operation of laws. *See* Savigny, *Treatise*, at 49. Savigny discussed both limits in the same volume under the title "Conflict of Laws and the Limits of their Operation in Respect of Place and Time."

81 *See, e.g.*, L. Brilmayer, "Interest Analysis and the Myth of Legislative Intent," 78 *Mich. L. Rev.* 392, 417 (1980) ("[D]omestic interpretation and conflicts interpretation are different enterprises altogether."); M. Rosenberg, "The Comeback of Choice of Law Rules," 81 *Colum. L. Rev.* 946, 947 (1981) (arguing that, in resorting to the domestic method, Currie "inescapably" implies that "the 'foreign elements' in a case do not call for a

incapable of pinpointing the policies underlying the conflicting rules of law.[82] They also argued that, even if such policies can be ascertained, they cannot help courts to delineate a law's intended territorial reach.[83]

To the extent Currie's critics deny the domestic method's ability to ascertain state policies, or at least those of the forum state, these criticisms are unjustified. "The most important lesson taught in the first year of law school is that an intelligent decision to apply or not to apply a legal rule depends upon knowing the reasons for the rule."[84] In this sense, Currie's domestic method is just another name for the teleological method,[85] which ought to be beyond reproach, at least among functionalist scholars. Ascertaining the *telos*, or purpose, of a law is more difficult in conflicts cases than in ordinary domestic cases, but is both a surmountable and worthy task.

Equally unjustified is the criticism of the teleological method's ability to delineate the intended spatial reach of the interpreted laws. The vitality of this method has never depended on proof of *actual* legislative intent, as critics assume. Without agreeing with Currie's method, or with his particular inferences about the spatial reach of laws, one can still accept that the spatial reach of laws is best determined by looking to their purpose and function. It is a separate matter that such a determination is only half of the process of actually resolving a conflicts problem. The other half, in which Currie's insights are much

---

distinctive mode of refereeing."). *See also* R.A. Leflar, "Choice-of-Law Statutes," 44 *Tenn. L. Rev.* 951, 954 (1977) ("The term 'statutory construction' is no more than a pretentious disguise for application of the court's conflicts law.").

82 *See, inter alia*, E.J. Bodenheimer, "The Need for a Reorientation in American Conflicts Law," 19 *Hastings L.J.* 731, 737 (1978); Brilmayer, "The Myth," *supra* previous note, at 399, 417, 424; P. Hay, "Reflections on Conflict-of-Laws Methodology: A Dialogue," 32 *Hastings L.J.* 1644, 1661 (1981); F.K. Juenger, "Conflict of Laws: A Critique of Interest Analysis," 32 *Am. J. Comp. L.* 1, 33-35 (1984); W. Reese, "Chief Judge Fuld and Choice of Law," 71 *Colum. L. Rev.* 548, 559-560 (1971); M. Rosenberg, "Two Views on *Kell v. Henderson*: An Opinion for the New York Court of Appeals," 67 *Colum. L. Rev.* 459, 463-464 (1967).

83 *See* Brilmayer, "The Myth," *supra*, at 393 ("[L]egislatures have no actual intent on territorial reach."); Juenger, "Critique," *supra* previous note, at 35 ("[P]olicies do not come equipped with labels proclaiming their spatial dimension."). For counter arguments, *see* H.H. Kay, "A Defense of Currie's Governmental Interest Analysis," 215 *Recueil des cours* 9, 117-129 (1989); R.A. Sedler, "Interest Analysis and Forum Preference in the Conflict of Laws: A Response to the 'New Crits,'" 34 *Mercer L. Rev.* 593, 606-620 (1983); R.A. Sedler, "Reflections on Conflict-of-Laws Methodology," 32 *Hastings L.J.* 1628, 1632-1635 (1981); R.J. Weintraub, "Interest Analysis in the Conflict of Laws as an Application of Sound Legal Reasoning," 35 *Mercer L. Rev.* 629, 630-634 (1984).

84 Weintraub, "Interest Analysis," *supra* previous note, at 631.

85 *See* H. Baade, "Counter-Revolution or Alliance for Progress? Reflections on Reading Cavers, The Choice-of-Law Process," 46 *Tex. L. Rev.* 141, 149 (1967) ("[G]overnmental interest analysis is merely one of the many applications of teleological interpretation. It seeks to determine the pertinence of rules of law to multiple-contact cases through an analysis of the purposes behind these rules.").

less inspiring, is to actually and rationally accommodate laws with overlapping spatial reach (that is, resolving true conflicts). I shall return to this point later.[86]

Having completely rejected the existing choice-of-law system, Currie had the sense to turn to something equally well-established but more flexible and resourceful – the domestic common law method. This opened the door to introducing functionalism into choice-of-law thinking, allowing a more individualized handling of cases and tempering the conflictual method by injecting it with considerations of substantive justice. Of all the elements of Currie's theory, this is the least problematic.

In conclusion, even when a conflict involves statutes (or common law rules) that do not declare their intended territorial reach, it is not difficult to determine whether application of that statute or rule would promote the policies or values of its state of origin. It is not difficult to see that the tax base of a state like Nevada, which depends heavily on the casino industry, would be adversely affected if that industry is subject to civil liability under the law of another state;[87] or that a state like Michigan, the home of the three largest U.S. auto makers, would be adversely affected if they are subject to punitive damages under the law of another state;[88] or that a country that depends heavily on its shipping industry would be adversely affected if that industry is subjected to American operating and compensation standards.[89] This *adverse impact* is the essence of the term state "interest."

---

86 *See infra* II.D.2.

87 Even the California court acknowledged this interest in *Bernhard v. Harrah's Club*, 546 P.2d 719 (Cal. 1976). *See id.* at 722 ("[I]t is clear that each state [California and Nevada] has an interest in the application of its respective law of liability and nonliability. It goes without saying that these interests conflict.").

88 *See, e.g., Kelly v. Ford Motor Co.*, 933 F. Supp. 465, 470 (E.D. Pa. 1996) (stating that Michigan had "a very strong interest" in applying its law denying punitive damages so as to ensure that "its domiciliary defendants are protected from excessive financial liability," and that by protecting companies such as Ford from punitive damages, "Michigan hopes to promote corporate migration into its economy ... [which] will enhance the economic climate and well being of the state ... by generating revenues"); *Ness v. Ford Motor Co.*, 1993 WL 996164 at *2 (N.D. Ill. July 20, 1993) ("Michigan has an interest in seeing that product-liability plaintiffs are not overcompensated, resulting in higher insurance premiums for Michigan manufacturers, higher costs, and lost jobs"); In re *Air Crash Disaster Near Chicago*, 644 F.2d 594, 614 (7th Cir. 1981) (emphasizing California's "substantial interest in the economic health of corporations ... which do business within its borders" and the ability of such corporations to "enhance[] the economic well-being of the state."). For discussion of Michigan's protectionism of three major automakers, *see* S.C. Symeonides, "Choice of Law in the American Courts in 1998: Twelfth Annual Survey," 47 *Am. J. Comp. L.* 327, 375-376 (1998), and the authorities cited therein.

89 *See* Symeonides, "Maritime Conflicts," at 224-225, 228, 247.

C *Re-conceptualizing State Interests*

In articulating the otherwise valid concept of state interests, Currie unfortunately used terms that imply that a "government" has an *active desire* to apply its law and, even worse, a proclivity to assert that desire in an aggressive, imperialistic, beggar-thy-neighbor fashion. Currie either erred or exaggerated. States do not have active desires with regard to the outcome of private disputes. But the policies, purposes, and values embodied in a state's law *can* be adversely affected when that law is *not* applied to a case the law was intended to reach. A state's "interest" in applying its law is simply a shorthand way of describing this *adverse* consequence. Whether one calls this an "interest" or "concern" or opts for a term such as "the most significant relationship," which the uninitiated may mistake for a mere geographical test, is a secondary matter. The bottom line is that states are *not* indifferent to the resolution of conflicts between their respective laws. Consequently, a choice-of-law analysis that fails to consider this factor is presumptively deficient.

This conclusion does not carry with it a wholesale, or even partial, subscription to Currie's particular value-system – especially the narrow, self-centered perspective he ascribed to the forum state, and his assumption that states are only interested in protecting their own citizens (the "personal law" principle). Currie's perspective and its corollaries are antithetical to the goals of private interstate and international law.[90] To paraphrase John Donne, *no state is an island*, even if it is geographically so.[91] A selfish pursuit of the forum's interests is inimical to individual justice and states' coexistence, and detrimental to the forum's own long-term interests.

D *Can an Interest-Based Approach Rationally Resolve Conflicts?*

In sum, Currie's basic premise that states have an interest in the outcome of multistate disputes between private persons accurately reflects contemporary reality. Nonetheless, Currie's articulation of those interests is intentionally provocative and unintentionally

90 *See, e.g.*, D. F. Cavers, *The Choice of Law Process* 151 n. 29 (1965) [hereinafter Cavers, *Process*] (asserting that some of Currie's prescriptions are "more appropriate to a tribal system of law than to that prevailing in the American Union."). Currie explained that his analysis did "not imply the ruthless pursuit of self-interest by the states," and did not preclude what he called "rational altruism." Currie, *Selected Essays* 185, 186. *See also id.* at 549 ("In a federal union such as ours there is no room for the cycle of discrimination, retaliation, and reciprocity. Each state may and should extend the benefits of its laws to foreigners, not merely with the hope but with the assurance that all other states will reciprocate as a matter of course."). However, Currie never retracted his personal-law principle, according to which a state's interest is confined to protecting only its own citizens. In short, Currie first elevated a faulty assumption into a choice-of-law principle and then relied on "rational altruism" and self-restraint to resolve the resulting problems and curtail the inevitable excesses.

91 J. Donne, "No Man is an Island, Meditation XVII," in *Devotions upon Emergent Occasions* 62 (1624).

chauvinistic. Properly conceived, state interests can be a good starting point for the judicial resolution of conflicts in the United States, and perhaps also in other common-law systems. Specifically, state interests provide the criteria for classifying conflicts cases into three analytically helpful categories—false conflicts, true conflicts, and "no interest" cases[92]—and for rationally resolving false conflicts. However, as explained below, an approach based solely on state interests encounters surmountable difficulties in true conflicts and insurmountable difficulties in "no-interest" cases.

1 False Conflicts

Because a false conflict is, by definition, a case in which only one state has an interest in applying its law, the application of that state's law (as Currie suggests) is the only sensible solution. This part of Currie's analysis is neither controversial nor controvertible. It is no wonder that all other modern approaches have embraced this solution, which is a significant improvement from the First Restatement. By basing the choice of law on the location of a single contact, rather than on the policies of the contact states, the Restatement often led to the random sacrifice of one state's interests without promoting the interests of another.[93] By contrast, Currie's solution to a false conflict effectuates the policies of the interested state *without* undermining any policies of the uninterested state.

This is by no means a small accomplishment. In the centuries-long history of PIL, progress has come in slow, tiny steps. Empowering the decision-maker to separate false conflicts from other conflicts, and to resolve false conflicts by applying the law of the only interested state, is one of few breakthroughs in the recent PIL history. This is true even after conceding, as one should, that reasonable minds can differ in defining a state's interest or on whether a particular case is in fact a false conflict.

2 True Conflicts

Currie's solution to true conflicts leaves as much to be desired as does his rationale. Currie contended that the only solution is to apply forum law, because a court *may not* subordinate

92 This tripartite categorization of conflicts, for which Currie deserves full credit, is analytically useful. However, the three labels Currie attached to the three categories are problematic because they forejudge the answer to the basic question (i.e., whether a state has an interest in applying its law to the particular case), a question that reasonable minds often answer differently. For this reason, the terms "direct" and "inverse" conflicts are preferable to Currie's second and third labels. Direct conflicts (Currie's "true conflicts") are those in which each involved state has a law that favors the party affiliated with that state. Inverse conflicts (Currie's "no-interest" cases) are those in which each state has a law that favors the party affiliated with the other state. These alternative terms objectively describe the content of each state's substantive law, without assuming the state does, or does not, have an interest in its application; further, they do not forejudge a court's categorization of the conflict or its ultimate outcome. *See* S.C. Symeonides & W.C. Perdue, *Conflict of Laws: American Comparative, International* 150-51 (3d ed. 2012).

93 *See* Currie, *Selected Essays,* 191. *See also id.* at 589-590.

the forum state's interests to those of another state.[94] Indeed, that very possibility impelled Currie to insist that judges should not even attempt to weigh the interests of the two states. His explanation is that judges have neither the constitutional power nor the necessary resources to weigh conflicting governmental interests, and should not be put in the position of having to subordinate the forum's interests. Currie contended that such weighing of interests is a "political function of a very high order ... that should not be committed to courts in a democracy."[95]

In light of Currie's proud adherence to the common-law tradition,[96] the above explanation is surprising. It assumes a conception of the judicial process that does not reflect the realities of the American common-law tradition, in which judges routinely evaluate and weigh conflicting social policies.[97] As Currie's friend Judge Roger Traynor, Chief Justice of California's supreme court, wrote, "[J]udicial responsibility ... connotes the recurring choice of one policy over another."[98] Currie's rationale also contradicts the basic premise of his theory, which assumes an activist judge in every other respect. For example, according to Currie's own analysis, a judge must identify and articulate the interests of the involved states in order to determine whether a conflict is a false or true conflict. The judicial application of this part of Currie's analysis suggests that the determination is no less subjective or politically sensitive than a weighing of interests. The two tasks differ only in degree. If judges are qualified and empowered to identify governmental interests, they neither lose nor abdicate that power when they encounter a true conflict.[99]

---

94 *See* Currie, "Comments on Babcock v. Jackson — A Recent Development in Conflict of Laws," 63 *Colum. L. Rev.* 1233, 1237-1238 (1963) ("In the absence of action by higher authority, each state must be conceded the *right* to apply its own laws for the reasonable effectuation of its own policies.") (emphasis added).

95 Currie, *Selected Essays*, 182. Currie also spoke of the "embarrassment of [a court] having to nullify the interests of its own sovereign." Currie, *Selected Essays* 278-279, 357; B. Currie, "The Disinterested Third State," 28 *Law & Contemp. Probs.* 754, 778 (1963).

96 *See* Currie, *Selected Essays*, 627 ("I am proud to associate myself with the common law tradition.").

97 *See* F.K. Juenger, "Choice of Law in Interstate Torts," 118 *U. Pa. L. Rev.* 200, 206-207 (1969) ("Ever since conflicts law first developed, courts did precisely what Currie would forbid them to do; no judge has ever been impeached for inventing or applying a choice of law rule that sacrifices forum interests.").

98 R.J. Traynor, "The Limits of Judicial Creativity," 63 *Iowa L. Rev.* 1, at 12. (1977). *See also id.* at 11 (rejecting the notion that "policy is a matter for the legislators alone.").

99 As Cavers put it, under Currie's analysis, the "[w]eighing of interests after interpretation is condemned: weighing of interests in interpretation, condoned, not to say, encouraged." D.F. Cavers, "Contemporary Conflicts in American Perspective," 131 *Recueil des cours* 75, 148 (1970). In one of his last writings, Currie advised that in some cases, the judge should subject the laws of the involved states to a more moderate and restrained interpretation, which could lead to a conclusion that one of those states is not as interested as it might appear. If so, this would be an apparent conflict in which the judge should apply the law of the other state. *See* Currie, "The Disinterested Third State," 28 *Law & Contemp. Probs.* 754, 763, 764 (1963). Currie unpersuasively asserted that the process of re-evaluating the two states' interests is qualitatively different from weighing them. *See* Currie, *Selected Essays* 759.

Fortunately, most courts that have adopted Currie's analysis have rejected his proscription of interest weighing. Instead, these courts openly and unapologetically weigh the conflicting state interests. This is what courts in the District of Columbia do,[100] and what New Jersey courts did before that state's Supreme Court abandoned Currie's approach in favor of the Restatement (Second).[101] The same is true of California courts, which invented another term for interest weighing: comparative impairment.[102] Rather than weighing state interests as such, California courts weigh the impairment that would result from not applying the law of a particular state. As Albert Ehrenzweig observed long ago, "All courts and writers who have professed acceptance of Currie's interest language have transformed it by indulging in that very weighing and balancing of interests from which Currie refrained."[103] Moreover, in many cases, these courts concluded that the stronger interest was that of the *foreign* state rather than that of the forum. This phenomenon suggests that, although Currie's analysis favors the *lex fori*, such bias is not an inherent characteristic of all interest-based approaches.

Thus, Currie's impasse in true conflicts can be surmounted by impartial state interest weighing, comparative impairment,[104] or "consequentialism."[105] The latter is the principle underlying the Louisiana choice-of-law codification of 1991,[106] and the last iteration of

---

100 *See, e.g.*, Kaiser-Georgetown Comm. *Health Plan, Inc. v. Stutsman*, 491 A.2d 502 (D.C. 1985); *Stutsman v. Kaiser Found. Health Plan*, 546 A.2d. 367 (D.C. 1988); *Cárdenas v. Muangman*, 998 A.2d 303 (D.C. 2010). *See also Biscoe v. Arlington County*, 738 F.2d 1352 (D.C. Cir. 1984); *Jaffe v. Pallotta Teamworks*, 374 F.3d 1223 (D.C. Cir. 2004).

101 *See, e.g.*, *Gantes v. Kason Corporation*, 679 A.2d 106 (N.J. 1996); *Eger v. E.I. Du Pont De Nemours Co.*, 539 A.2d 1213 (N.J. 1988).

102 *See Bernhard v. Harrah's Club*, 546 P.2d 719 (Cal. 1976) (adopting Baxter's comparative impairment approach as the method for resolving cases that interest analysis classifies as true conflicts). Baxter explained his approach in W.F. Baxter, Choice of Law and the Federal System, 16 *Stan. L. Rev.* 1 (1963). For subsequent applications of this mix, *see Offshore Rental Co. v. Continental Oil Co*, 583 P.2d 721 (Cal. 1978); *Kearney v. Salomon Smith Barney, Inc.*, 137 P.3d 914 (Cal. 2006); *McCann v. Foster Wheeler LLC.*, 225 P.3d 516 (Cal. 2010).

103 A. Ehrenzweig, "A Counter-Revolution in Conflicts Law?," 80 *Harv. L. Rev.* 377, 389 (1966). Currie's response was sharp and short: "I do not care whether courts undertake to weigh and balance conflicting interests or not". But when they do, "such action can find its justification in politics, not in jurisprudence." Currie, *Selected Essays*, 600-601. For a more restrained response, *see id.* at 183, 274.

104 *See* W.F. Baxter, "Choice of Law and the Federal System," 16 *Stan. L. Rev.* 1 (1963).

105 This term originated in theology to describe a doctrine postulating that the morality of an act is to be judged solely by its consequences. In choice-of-law, consequentialism stands for the proposition that the quality of a choice-of-law decision is to be judged by the consequences it produces on the interests and values embodied in the conflicting laws.

106 *See* S.C. Symeonides, "The Conflicts Book of the Louisiana Civil Code: Civilian, American, or Original?," 83 *Tul. L. Rev.* 1041, 1049-54 (2009). For the differences between the Louisiana approach and Baxter's and California's comparative impairment approach, *see* S.C. Symeonides, "Louisiana's New Law of Choice of Law for Tort Conflicts: An Exegesis," 66 *Tul. L. Rev.* 677, 691-92 (1992).

Russell Weintraub's approach;[107] namely, selecting the law of the state whose interests would suffer the most serious adverse consequences if its law were not applied.[108]

The common denominator between (1) resolving false conflicts by applying the law of the only interested state, and (2) resolving true conflicts by applying the law of the state with the greatest impairment, is the principle of *accommodation* of state interests. Rather than thinking in terms of *advancing* the interests of one state at the expense of those of another, the decision maker should aspire to avoid frustrating the interests of the state with the most to lose from an adverse choice of law. In false conflicts, that state is the only interested state. In true conflicts, it is the state with the strongest interest. Accommodation is a unilateralist principle in that, rather than denying the existence of state interests, it openly acknowledges them. The fact that it attempts to accommodate these interests makes it a benevolent or accommodative unilateralism, as opposed to Currie's aggressive, imperialistic version.[109]

3 No-Interest Cases

Ironically, no-interest cases are more problematic for interest analysts than true conflicts. It is perfectly logical and consistent to resolve a true conflict by applying the law of the state with the strongest interest, or whose interests would otherwise suffer the most serious impairment. But what is one to do in the no-interest cases? Try to find the least disinterested state? Put another way, Currie's analysis, as it is built around the notion of state interests, comes to an impasse when neither state has an interest. In order to resolve the conflict, one must look for options outside the framework of interest analysis instead of simply recalibrating state interests or searching for phantom common policies. In this sense, Currie's solution of applying the law of the forum as the residual law, is precisely that—a solution that lies *outside* the framework of interest analysis.

Once it is understood that the solution to the no-interest conundrum must be sought outside the framework of interest analysis, other options become more palatable. Currie's

---

107 *See* R.J. Weintraub, *Commentary on the Conflict of Laws*, 371 (5th ed. 2006) (proposing a "consequences-based approach" that "chooses law with knowledge of the content of the laws of each of the [involved] states ... [and] seeks to minimize the consequences that any such state is likely to experience if its law is not applied."). *See also id.* at 380 (stating that the Louisiana codification is based on such an approach).

108 For an example of such a resolution of true conflicts, *see* Articles 3543 and 3544 of the Louisiana codification. These articles provide that, subject to some qualifications, cases in which the tortfeasor's conduct occurred in one state, while the victim's injury occurred in another state with a higher standard of conduct or financial protection for the victim, are governed by the law of the latter state if the tortfeasor should have foreseen that the injury would occur in that state.

109 *See* S.C. Symeonides, "Accommodative Unilateralism as a Starting Premise in Choice of Law, in H-E. Rasmussen-Bonne, R. Freer, W. Lüke & W. Weitnauer (eds.), *Balancing of Interests: Liber Amicorum Peter Hay* 417-434 (2005).

lex fori solution is practical and efficient, but it should be compared to other options, such as (1) a return to territorialism, which was the established system prior to the advent of interest analysis; or (2) a resort to material justice considerations.

Interestingly, and despite contrary assumptions or expectations, judges have not found Currie's *lex fori* solution appealing in no-interest cases. A telling example is presented by tort cases in which the parties are domiciled in different states, and both the conduct and injury occurred either in the tortfeasor's home state (which has a law protecting the victim), or in the victim's home state (with a law protecting the tortfeasor). In these cases, the courts applied the law of the state with the three contacts, even when it was not the forum state.[110] The Louisiana and Oregon codifications have adopted the same solution.[111]

E *Summary*

Currie was essentially correct in postulating that (1) multistate disputes between private parties implicate the interests of the states that have significant contacts with the dispute, in addition to the interests of the parties; and (2) in order to identify those interests, one must examine the substantive laws of the involved states, ascertain their underlying purposes or policies, and determine whether they are implicated in the case at hand.

However, the way in which Currie conceived and articulated these interests conjures Cold War memories or conditions of open economic warfare between states. We should not hesitate to pinpoint and castigate this fact, especially in these days of coarsened international discourse precipitated primarily by the xenophobic rhetoric and actions of the individual who happens to occupy the White House at the time of this writing.

Properly conceived, a state's interest *in the realm of conflict of laws* lies not in selfishly maximizing its gains to the detriment of other states, but in avoiding an adverse impact on its strongly held policies or values. This difference in conception is not as consequential in false conflicts, which implicates only one state's interests, but it is problematic in true conflicts, especially because of Currie's proscription of interest weighing. Such proscription was another error of Currie's, which can be (and has been) corrected by courts that follow his approach. The correction can consist of either comparing the strength of the conflicting state interests or, better yet, as suggested here, by weighing the adverse consequences that the choice-of-law decision would have on the interests of each involved state, and applying the law of the state that would suffer the most by an adverse decision. This leaves conflicts

110 *See* Symeonides, *Oxford Commentaries*, 204-18.
111 *See* La. Civ. Code art. 3544(2)(a); Or. Rev. Stat. § 15.440(3(b).

that cannot be resolved through the previous two steps, including cases in which none of the involved states has an interest in applying their law. In those cases, the governing law should be chosen by resorting to other choice-of-law criteria, including territorial considerations.

III Not "Only in America": Recognition of State Interests Elsewhere

A Not for Export

To readers outside the United States, the preceding discussion may appear as nothing more than an American intramural squabbling that has nothing to contribute to the international discourse. Indeed, many foreign critics view Currie's approach and the surrounding debates as just another American peculiarity. For instance, Michael Bogdan concludes:

> [E]ven if the governmental interest analysis could be regarded as suitable for conflicts of law within the United States (which, however, is very doubtful), it can hardly be transplanted into conflicts between the legal systems of completely independent countries with substantial differences not only in the contents of their substantive legal rules but also in their social structure and socially accepted values.[112]

One can question some of the premises of Bogdan's statement, but not his conclusion that Currie's approach *as such* is not for export. Currie never made, nor could he make, such a claim – if only because *he didn't care*.[113] However, the question here is not whether Currie's approach is transplantable elsewhere, but whether his core notion that states have an interest in the outcome of multistate disputes between private parties is as alien to other legal systems as many PIL scholars outside the United States assume; in other words, whether PIL is truly private in the sense that Gerhard Kegel described it. The most realistic way of answering this question is by turning to the official and real world of legislation.

112 M. Bogdan, "Private International Law as Component of the Law of the Forum," 348 *Recueil des cours* 9 63 (2011) [hereinafter Bogdan, "Law of the Forum"].

113 *See* S.C. Symeonides, *An Outsider's View of the American Approach to Choice of Law: Comparative Observations on Current American and Continental Conflicts Doctrine* 32-34 (1980).

B *The Obvious: Unilateralist Tools*

Most PIL codifications enacted in the last fifty years employ a whole panoply of devices designed to protect specific values or interests of the forum state in the international arena. In other publications, I provide detailed documentation of this pervasive phenomenon.[114] First, the majority of foreign PIL codifications employ multiple inward-looking unilateral rules in fields traditionally viewed as falling within the private law sphere, such as torts, contracts, multiple nationalities, capacity, marriage, divorce, adoption, maintenance, successions, and property.[115] Second, at least 35 PIL codifications enacted in the last fifty years, three EU Regulations, and nine international conventions contain *general* provisions giving priority to the forum's mandatory rules, which by definition embody important public interests,[116] while 22 codifications, two EU Regulations, and six conventions expressly authorize the application of the mandatory rules of both the forum state and a *third* foreign state, in addition to the state of the *lex causae*.[117] Third, many states insert localizing rules in substantive "private-law" statutes, mandating the application of those statutes to cases that have specified contacts with the forum state, in derogation of choice-of-law rules contained in PIL codifications.[118]

The widespread use of so many and diverse unilateralist devices confirms that contemporary legislatures understand that many categories of conflicts cases implicate not only the private interests of the disputing parties, but also *public* or *state* interests. This should not be surprising. Legislation is the formal expression of a sovereign's will, which in a democracy is the collective will of its people. If a statute regulating domestic cases is meant to protect and promote broad societal interests (among other values), why should a choice-of-law rule or statute intended for multistate cases ignore those interests?[119] A survey of recent PIL codifications and other statutes emphatically answers this question in favor of those

114 *See* Symeonides, *Idealism*, 143-79.

115 *See id.* 143-64.

116 For a table listing these codifications, see S.C. Symeonides, *Codifying Choice of Law Around the World: An International Comparative Analysis*, 305-06 (2014) [hereinafter Symeonides, *Codifying Choice of Law*]. This count does not include codifications that provide for mandatory rules only as limitations to party autonomy, or states that recognize mandatory rules only through special statutes, judicial decisions, or academic doctrine.

117 *See id.* Obviously, if a mandatory rule is part of the *lex causae*, that rule applies as part of the *lex causae*. It applies because of, rather than "irrespective" of, the choice-of-law rule that designates the *lex causae*.

118 Symeonides, *Idealism*, 172-79.

119 According to Jürgen Basedow, "[W]here States … consider certain values and legal institutions as foundational … [they] will usually take a unilateral approach: all they are interested in is the effectiveness and the scope of their own regulations. They rarely look abroad for corresponding rules in other countries." J. Basedow, "The Law of Open Societies: Private Ordering and Public Regulation in the Conflict of Laws," 360 *Recueil des cours* 9, at 416 (2013). Basedow also notes that "there is now a new and increasingly discernible trend in Western societies to impose their own values and principles, sometimes in the guise of fundamental or human rights claiming universal respect." *Id.* at 448.

interests.[120] To quote one European author: Throughout history, "[w]hether cloaked in terms of territoriality, public policy, governmental interests, or *Sonderanknüpfung*, the protection of national public interests has always outweighed any other choice-of-law consideration."[121]

C *The Less Obvious: Multilateral But Non-Neutral Rules*

Moreover, a careful review of PIL codifications reveals that states protect their interests not only through unilateral rules and other unilateralist devices, but also through certain multilateral rules. As Michael Bogdan acknowledges:

> [T]he bilateral nature of a conflict rule does not guarantee that the rule treats foreign law and the *lex fori* alike, even though such equality of treatment is normally considered desirable as a matter of principle. A bilateral conflict rule may expressly require more for the application of foreign law than for the application of the *lex fori* ..., and it may also discriminate against foreign law in a covert way.[122]

Indeed, contemporary codifiers know how to draft multilateral choice-of-law rules that appear facially neutral, but which are calculated to lead to the application of forum law more frequently than foreign law. Even during the idealistic period of the late nineteenth and early twentieth centuries, it was widely acknowledged that the debate on whether to use nationality or domicile as a connecting factor for status and succession issues, though phrased in lofty deontological terms, was essentially a pragmatic debate about conflicting national interests of countries with emigrating populations and those with immigrating populations.[123] Countries with emigrating populations opted for nationality as the connect-

---

120 *See* Symeonides, *Codifying Choice of Law*, 289-344.

121 T.M. de Boer, "Living Apart Together: The Relationship Between Public and Private International Law," 57 *Neth. Int'l L. Rev.* 183, 204 (2010); *See also* Basedow, *Open Societies*, at 469 (detecting "an inclination of the courts to identify numerous mandatory rules and principles of the lex fori with public policy or overriding mandatory provisions which have to be enforced at any cost"), and *id.* at 448 (characterizing as a "political function" the courts' determination of "whether the imperative norms of the forum State are affected by the facts of a pending case and whether they are opposed to the decision of the case under foreign law.").

122 Bogdan, "Law of the Forum," 86.

123 *See, e.g.*, S. Vrellis, "Rapport grec," in S.C. Symeonides (ed.), *Private International Law at the End of the 20th Century: Progress or Regress?* 247-48 (2000) ("Sous certains aspects, le choix du législateur en ce qui concerne le facteur de rattachement prépondérant, qui reste encore en Grèce ... la nationalité, est un choix imposé par le souci de satisfaire aux intérêts nationaux ou étatiques, à une époque où la Grèce était un pays d'émigration, donc un pays qui cherchait à maintenir ses liens avec ses ressortissants qui s'installaient à l'étranger ainsi qu'avec les descendants."); S. Vrellis, "Introductory Observations to Private International Law in Greece, 82, in A.S. Georgiadis & M.P. Stathopoulos (eds.), *Civil Code, Article by Article Interpretation*, v. IA 2016 (in Greek).

ing factor, in order to maintain a bond with their emigrating citizens; by contrast, countries with immigrating populations chose domicile as a means of assimilating the immigrants living in their territory, while also avoiding the application of foreign laws. As Louis de Winter noted, "Hardly anybody will dispute nowadays that the romantic grounds advanced by Mancini for the application of the nationality principle were inspired by political motives."[124] Of course, the same observation could apply to the proponents of domicile.[125] "Political" is not a dirty word in this context, but one who prefers more sanitized or nuanced expressions would speak in terms of state policies or interests.

To provide a realistic, contemporary hypothesis, suppose that for products liability conflicts: (1) country *A*, a net exporter of large quantities of products, has pro-manufacturer substantive law and adopts a choice-of-law rule calling for the application of the law of the producer's home state; and (2) country *B*, a net importer, adopts a rule giving consumers a choice between the laws of the victim's home state, the place of injury, the place of the product's acquisition, or the producer's home state. Both of these rules are bilateral, and thus ostensibly neutral. However, in their actual operation, the first rule would serve the exporting country's interest in protecting its manufacturers through the application of its pro-manufacturer substantive law, while the second would serve the importing country's interest in protecting its consumers by affording them several choices for the applicable law.

Many countries that are net importers of products have adopted pro-consumer choice-of-law rules similar to the hypothetical rule of country *B*.[126] Tunisia, for example, provides the consumer with a choice from among the laws of the defendant's principal place of business or domicile, the state in which the product was acquired, the victim's habitual residence, and the state of injury.[127] The codifications of Azerbaijan, Belarus, Kazakhstan, Kyrgyzstan, Tajikistan, and Uzbekistan allow the first three choices,[128] while the Quebec codification gives consumers "only" two choices: (1) the state of the defendant's principal place of business or, in the absence thereof, habitual residence; and (2) the state in which

124 L.I. de Winter, "Nationality or Domicile? The Present State of Affairs," 128 *Recueil des cours* 344, 400 (1969).

125 *See* F.K. Juenger, "American and European Conflicts Law," 30 *Am. J. Comp. L.* 117, 130 (1982) ("Whatever one might say about attempts by emigration countries to retain some hold over their citizens abroad, nations that attract large numbers of immigrants clearly court trouble if they disregard the very real nexus that group of their population has with their new homeland. Stubborn insistence on nationality as the only legal tie that matters is bound to swamp their courts with foreign-law issues.").

126 *See* Symeonides, *Codifying Choice of Law*, 96-98.

127 *See* Tunisian PIL codif. art. 72.

128 *See* Azerbaijan PIL codif. art. 27; Belarus PIL codif. art. 1130; Kazakhstan PIL codif. art. 1118; Kyrgyzstan PIL codif. art. 1203; Tajikistan PIL codif. art. 1227; Ukrainian PIL codif. art. 50; Uzbekistan PIL codif. art. 1195.

the product was acquired.[129] However, the same codification also provides that Quebec law "imperative[ly]" applies to products liability actions for injury outside (or within) Quebec "as a result of exposure to or the use of raw materials ... originating in Quebec."[130] Thus, Quebec protects Quebec consumers injured by foreign producers *as well as* certain Quebec producers injuring foreign consumers.

No country has adopted a rule that favors manufacturers as blatantly as the hypothetical rule of country *A* described above. However, one major exporter—Japan—has come very close. The new Japanese codification calls for the application of the law of the state of the product's delivery and, if delivery in that state was not foreseeable, then the law of the state of the producer's principal establishment.[131] Looked at in isolation, this rule does not unduly favor Japanese manufacturers because it does subject them to the laws of the states in which their products are foreseeably delivered. However, the protectionist element surfaces in two unilateral rules to which this rule is subject. The first rule is a double-actionability rule that provides that when foreign law governs a tort, the victim may not claim damages or "any other remedies" under that law if the injurious conduct is not "unlawful" under Japanese law.[132] This means, for example, that if an erroneous description of the product's qualities is not "unlawful" under Japanese law, but is unlawful under the otherwise applicable foreign law, the consumer would not be entitled to any remedy in Japan. The second unilateral rule provides that, even if the injurious conduct is unlawful under both foreign law and Japanese law, the victim "may not claim any greater recovery of damages or any other remedies than those available under Japanese law."[133] Thus, a Japanese manufacturer may not be forced to provide greater relief or pay higher damages than those provided by Japanese law.[134]

Rome II avoids a pro-defendant rule like the Japanese formula, as well as an overtly pro-plaintiff rule like those previously adopted in countries such as Italy and Switzerland, which give plaintiffs two choices on the applicable law. Instead, Rome II adopts a complex provision, Article 5, which is based on a sequential combination of contacts and cascading connecting factors. On its face, Article 5 seems perfectly neutral. Nonetheless, this Article leads to the application of the law of the victim's habitual residence in the majority of

---

129 Quebec PIL codif. art. 3128.

130 Quebec PIL codif. art. 3129. For a critique of this article and Article 3151, *see* H.P. Glenn, "La guerre de l'amiante," 80 *Rev. critique dr. int'l priv.* 41, 59 (1991).

131 *See* Japanese PIL codif. art. 18.

132 Japanese PIL codif. art. 22(1).

133 Japanese PIL codif. art. 22(2).

134 The converse phenomenon occurs when a country that has a pro-consumer substantive law makes it unavailable to foreign consumers.

cases.[135] This too is a seemingly neutral result, but it may not be so in its actual operation. When the plaintiff is a resident of an EU country with a generous pro-consumer law (e.g., France) and the manufacturer is based in a state with a pro-manufacturer law (e.g., Germany), the plaintiff will be protected under French law. But if the plaintiff is a habitual resident of, for instance, the Central African Republic, the same Article will ensure that the German defendant will be held accountable (or perhaps unaccountable) under the lower standards of the plaintiff's foreign residence. Thus, like the Quebec rules described above, this seemingly neutral, bilateral rule protects EU consumers injured by foreign (or EU) manufacturers, and EU manufacturers whose products injure foreign consumers. It confirms the astute observation that "[a]n apparently blind choice of law rule … can hide a firm substantive policy goal,"[136] which some call a state interest.

To be sure, Rome II does not use the term "state interest." For example, its Preamble describes Rome II's goal as "ensur[ing] a reasonable balance between the interests of [the *parties*, i.e.,] the person claimed to be liable and the person who has sustained damage."[137] However, closer examination reveals that Rome II recognizes that many tort conflicts implicate not only the interests of the litigants but also broader societal, public, and (thus) state interests. For example, with regard to products liability, recital 20 of Rome II speaks of the policies of "fairly spreading the risks … protecting consumers' health, stimulating innovation, securing undistorted competition and facilitating trade."[138] With regard to unfair competition, recital 21 speaks of the need to "protect competitors, consumers and the general public and ensure that the market economy functions properly."[139] Recital 25, concerning environmental torts, provides that the need for a "high level of [environmental] protection" and the "principle that the polluter pays" justify a choice-of-law rule "discriminating in favour of the person sustaining the damage."[140] Finally, recital 31 recognizes the need to impose certain restrictions on the parties' power to choose the governing law in order to protect weaker parties.[141]

More importantly, some of Rome II's dispositive articles can only be explained in terms of public (state) interests, rather than private interests. Besides Article 26, which codifies

135 *See* S.C. Symeonides, "Rome II and Tort Conflicts: A Missed Opportunity," 56 *Am. J. Comp. L.* 173, 207-09 (2008).

136 M. Fallon & J. Meeusen, "Belgian Report," in S. Symeonides (ed.), *Progress or Regress?* 112. *See also* F. Pocar & C. Honorati, Italian Report, in Symeonides, *Progress or Regress?* 289 ("[T]he use of a specific connecting factor could achieve (or jeopardize) certain results of substantive law.").

137 Rome II, recital (16).

138 Rome II, recital (20).

139 Rome II, recital (21).

140 Rome II, recital (25).

141 Rome II, recital (31).

the traditional *ordre public* exception, and Article 16, which allows the forum to interpose its own mandatory rules, many other provisions of Rome II are designed to serve specific substantive polices. The clearest example is Article 7, which in cross-border environmental torts serves the substantive policy of the "polluter pays" by allowing the plaintiff to choose the more favorable law of either the state of conduct or the state of injury.[142] Other less obvious examples include Articles 6(4) and 8(3), which prohibit choice-of-law agreements in cases of unfair competition, restriction to competition, and infringement of intellectual property rights; Article 14(2)-(3), which prohibits choice-of-law clauses to the extent they violate certain mandatory rules of a non-chosen state or of the EU; and Article 14(1)(b), which allows pre-tort choice-of-law clauses, though only in contracts between commercial parties and subject to other limitations.

D Constitutionalization of PIL

Another development that has blurred the private-public line is the constitutionalization of PIL in many European countries. This development began in 1971, with the well-known decision of the German Federal Constitutional Court known as the *Spanierbeschluss* (the "Spaniard's case"),[143] which involved the right of a Spanish national domiciled in Germany to marry a German divorcee. At that time, Spanish law prohibited divorce and did not allow the marriage. The Court held that the fact that German choice-of-law rules required the application of Spanish law was not a permissible ground on which to deny the parties the fundamental right to marry guaranteed by Germany's Basic Law. This meant that the lower court should either refuse to apply Spanish law by aligning the *ordre public* exception with the Basic Law, or directly grant this constitutional right to the involved parties. In either case, the clear message was that the public values or interests embodied in the Basic Law trumped the principles of PIL.

The *Spanierbeschluss* was a harbinger of many similar decisions by both national courts and later the European Court of Human Rights.[144] For example, in 1982, the German Federal Court of Justice (*Bundesgerichtshof*) held the German choice-of-law rules giving priority to the national law of the husband in family law disputes unconstitutional.[145] In

---

142 For discussion of this article, *see* S.C. Symeonides, "Rome II and Tort Conflicts: A Missed Opportunity," 56 *Am. J. Comp. L.* 173, 209-11 (2008).

143 *See* 31 BVerfGE 58 (4 May 1971).

144 For expert discussion, *see* P. Kinsch, "Droits de l'homme, droits fondamentaux et droit international privé," 318 *Recueil des cours* 9, 226-287 (2005); P. Kinsch, "Choice of Law Rules and the Prohibition of Discrimination under the European Convention on Human Rights," 29 *Ned. Int'l PrivR.* 19 (2011). *See also* L.R. Kiestra, *The Impact of the European Convention on Human Rights on Private International Law* (2014).

145 *See* 86 BGHZ 57 (8 December 1982).

1987, the Italian Constitutional Court held to the same effect with regard to Italy's choice-of-law rules.[146] As a knowledgeable human rights scholar observed at the time, "Today, the forum's rules determining the applicable law are not immune from scrutiny under constitutional or human rights law."[147]

In the meantime, the transformation of the European Economic Community into the European Union brought about a federalization of some parts of European PIL, and a constitutionalization of others. One of the consequences of the latter development is that the principle of nondiscrimination and other fundamental rights, as defined at the Union level, now preempt national choice-of-law rules and thus "overcome both the national and the private character of classical choice of law."[148] One example of this development is the 2003 decision of the European Court of Justice (ECJ) in the *Garcia Avello* case.[149] The Court held that children with dual Belgian and Spanish citizenship residing in Belgium were entitled to use their dual surname under Spanish law, even though the Belgian choice-of-law rule required the application of Belgian law. In *Grunkin-Paul*, the child was a German citizen born in Denmark to German parents, and was registered in Denmark under a hyphenated surname combining both parents' surnames according to Danish law. The ECJ held that the child had a right to have his hyphenated surname registered in Germany, even though the German choice-of-law rule required the application of German law, which did not allow the double surname under those circumstances.[150]

A great deal more can be said about the constitutionalization of PIL, but for the limited purposes of this discussion, I conclude with Horatia Muir Watt's observation that this phenomenon entails a "reversal of the relationship between the public and the private spheres" and "the reconnection of private international law to a political (public) horizon."[151]

146 *See* Corte cost. 26 February (5 March) 1987, No 71 Foro it., I, 2316 (1987).

147 P. Kinsch, "Human Rights and Private International Law," in Basedow, et al. (eds.), *Encyclopedia of PIL* (2017).

148 R. Michaels, "The New European Choice-of-Law Revolution," 82 *Tul. L. Rev.* 1607, 1625 (2008).

149 Case C-148/02, *Garcia Avello v. État Belge*, 2003 E.C.R. I-11, 613.

150 Case C-353/06, *Grunkin-Paul v. Standesamt Niebüll* (14 October 2008). For an extensive, thoughtful discussion of this case, as well as *Garcia Avello, see* M. Lehman, "What's in a Name? Grunkin-Paul and Beyond," 10 *Ybk. Priv. Int'l L.* 135 (2008).

151 H. Muir Watt (ed.), *Private International Law and Public Law* xvii (vol. 1, 2015).

Conclusions

As the above discussion illustrates, the notion that PIL is private law in the sense described by Gerhard Kegel is riddled with innumerable exceptions, even in Europe. Today, forum-protective rules exist in virtually every country. They may be methodologically or statistically 'exceptional,' but they are too numerous to be dismissed. They are employed not only in public-law fields, such as antitrust, but also in fields such as contracts, property, successions, marriage, divorce, and maintenance. Moreover, they protect not only economic interests of the enacting state, but also certain strongly held societal values and beliefs. For example, ensuring gender equality in marriage, as the Dutch and Belgian codifications do,[152] does not protect an economic interest but it does promote a society's sense of equality and freedom to marry. Finally, because these rules are statutory, courts have no choice but to apply them.

That contemporary PIL codifiers find it necessary to employ so many tools for the protection of national interests blurs the public-private law distinction that used to be so entrenched in European law. "[E]ven contract law, the most emblematic area of the liberal legal framework for the market economy, can hardly be seen to stand alone from public regulation and enforcement."[153] As Michel Rosenfeld notes:

> [I]f government departs more and more from a purely mediating role, and replaces freedom of contract with a contract law regime replete with directives and restrictions in the name of the public good, or, in other words, if contract law becomes increasingly paternalistic, then eventually it might appear to confound or cross the line between private and public law.[154]

Today, many European authors recognize that:
- "Economic regulatory policies are not a monopoly of public law," and there is at least an "intermingling of private and public interests."[155]
- "The State's concern for public welfare and the economic order has extended to relations between private parties" and has "reduced the significance of the distinction between

152 *See* Dutch PIL codif. art. 60; Belgian PIL codif. art. 46.
153 H. Muir Watt (ed.), *Private International Law and Public Law,* at xviii (vol. 1, 2015).
154 M. Rosenfeld, "Rethinking the Boundaries Between Public Law and Private Law for the Twenty First Century: An Introduction," 11 *Int'l J. Con. L.* 125, 126 (2013).
155 H. Muir Watt, "Choice of Law in Integrated and Interconnected Markets: A Matter of Political Economy," 9 *Colum. J. Eur. L.* 383 (2003). For an extensive discussion of these ideas and relevant authorities, *see* H. Muir Watt, "Aspects économiques du droit international privé," 307 *Recueil des cours* 25 *et seq.* (2005).

'*ius quod ad statum rei Romanae*' and '*ius quod ad singulorum utilitatem spectat.*'"[156]
"Public and private law have become increasingly interwoven."[157]

- "The old dichotomies between public law and private law ... are gradually fading," and PIL "is not exclusively concerned with international relationships between private parties."[158]
- "[P]rivate law is not as private as some may be tempted to think. Being law it reflects interests of society as a whole."[159]
- "[C]onflict rules ... are normally enacted and applied in the forum country's own interest and have the task of advancing its policies"[160] and "serve in principle the interests of the forum country rather than the interests of other countries."[161]
- "The forum state, as the author of conflicts rule, is inspired by its own regulatory interests."[162]

Frank Vischer, the principal drafter of the Swiss PIL codification, conceded as much. Although he posited that "the safeguard of the interests of individuals" should be the primary concern of PIL, Vischer also noted that "public interests are also involved. Social concern, as for instance the protection of the weak, has led to a greater involvement of the State in private law relations. The individual cannot escape the influence of the State through private international law."[163] Vischer candidly concluded that PIL is "an instrument often used for furthering State policies and advancing solutions which correspond best with the national notion of justice, an instrument which States do not easily renounce,"

156 Vischer, "General Course on Private International Law," 232 *Recueil des cours* 9, 150 (1992) (*quoting* Ulpian, Dig. 1.1.2).

157 *Id.*

158 T.M. de Boer, "Living Apart Together: The Relationship Between Public and Private International Law," 57 *Neth. Int'l L. Rev.* 183, 195 (2010). *See also* C.W. Fassberg, "Realism and Revolution in Conflict of Laws: In with a Bang and Out with a Whimper," 163 *U. Pa. L. Rev.* 1919, 1937 (2015) ("Recognizing the policy implications of private law rules challenges the traditional assumption that choice of law deals only with private law and that private and public law are clearly distinct.").

159 A.V.M. Struycken, "Coordination and Co-Operation in Respectful Disagreement: General Course in Private International Law," 311 *Recueil des cours* 33 (2004). *See also* B. Audit, "Le droit internationale privé en quête d'universalité," 305 *Recueil des cours* 9, 477 (2003) ("Conçu dans un environnement philosophique assimilant le droit privé à un espace de liberté, la méthode de la règle de conflit a évolué à mesure que le droit privé devenait plus finaliste ou dirigiste.").

160 Bogdan, "Law of the Forum," 64-65.

161 *Id.* at 46. However, Bogdan strongly disagrees with Currie's assumptions about the forum's interests. *See id.* at 75-77.

162 A. Bucher, "La dimension sociale du droit international privé," 341 *Recueil des cours* 9, 170 (2009) ("L'Etat du for, auteur de la règle de conflit, s'inspire de son propre intérêt de régulation quant à la loi applicable aux situations internationales."). *See also* S. Vrellis, "Introductory Observations," 85 ("Conflicts rules express and effectuate policies determined by the values and goals of the legal order of the forum state.").

163 Vischer, "General Course," at 31.

and that "[t]he antinomy between the source and the objective persists and will probably continue to do so in the near future."[164]

As another inside observer of the European PIL scene recently wrote:

> PIL is undergoing a metamorphosis: from a discipline which presented itself traditionally as a fairly isolated discipline with its own nature PIL is becoming a discipline whose function seems to be related to policy considerations that often have their place in essence outside PIL. With this PIL seems more and more to lose the character of neutrality. PIL is challenged to leave the cocoon position in which it had traditionally nestled down.[165]

In conclusion, PIL is no longer as "private," apolitical, or neutral as Savigny perceived it. His perception was justified by the conditions prevailing during his time, but those conditions barely outlasted the nineteenth century. As Jürgen Basedow noted, "[T]he rise of the interventionist and welfare state of the twentieth century has profoundly changed the model of society underlying Savigny's propositions."[166]

If PIL is not "private" in the sense described by Kegel, states cannot be apathetic spectators in conflicts cases. States are *not indifferent* to the outcome of multistate disputes between private persons as the classical school presumed.

At the same time, states are not as selfish as Currie finds them to be. The use above of the italicized double negative is intentional. It signals the difference between Currie's conception of state interests and the reconceptualization of those interests as suggested above.[167] There

164 *Id.* at 22.

165 V. Van Den Eeckhout, "The Instrumentalisation of Private International Law - Quo Vadis? Rethinking the 'Neutrality' of Private International Law in an Era of Globalisation and Europeanisation of Private International Law," in J.S. Bergé, S. Francq & M. Gardenes Santiago (eds.), *Boundaries of European Private International Law. Les frontières de droit international privé européen. Las fronteras del derecho internacional privado europea* 387, 391 (2015).

166 Basedow, *Open Societies*, at 47. *See id.* at 46-47:
In the middle of the nineteenth century, when liberal capitalism reached its peak and Savigny wrote his treatise, State interventions into economic and social life were indeed increasingly renounced and became exceptional. Consequently, Savigny did not write more than a very short chapter of seven pages on what he called "statutes of a strict and positive, mandatory nature ..." ... Of course, the rise of the interventionist and welfare state of the twentieth century has profoundly changed the model of society underlying Savigny's propositions. The public good is no longer perceived as exclusively flowing from the unhindered interaction of private actors, but is very often defined and directly targeted by State legislation. There are considerable differences between the laws of the various countries, and many of them are implemented by mandatory private law or even by public law interventions. Due to the conditions of his time, Savigny turned a blind eye to this part of the legal order.

167 *See supra* II.C.

is a difference between saying that a state is interested in applying its law at any cost, and saying that a state, *in certain cases*, may be adversely affected if its law is not applied. The difference is not only psychological – it has methodological implications as well. A method such as Currie's version of ethnocentric unilateralism is unnecessarily bellicose, potentially unfair to private litigants, and counterproductive in the long run.

Even so, the realization that states have interests in PIL disputes is not something worthy of celebration. For it means, as Spyros Vrellis put it, that PIL has "lost its innocence."[168] However, although this loss of innocence is regrettable, it would be even more regrettable if we pretended that it has not occurred. A good understanding of reality is the first pre-condition for successfully addressing the problem at hand. As we proceed into the twenty-first century, we can expect that states will, even more boldly, assert their interest in multistate private-law disputes. Our discipline can facilitate the functioning of the international legal order by recognizing the existence of state interests, ascertaining whether and when they truly conflict, and articulating the principles and mechanisms that will provide a reasonable accommodation between these interests.

168 S. Vrellis, "Rapport grec," in S. Symeonides (ed.), *Progress or Regress?*, 247 ("Le droit international privé a perdu son innocence.").

Maastricht Law Series

The Maastricht Law Series is created in 2018 by Boom juridisch and Eleven International Publishing in association with the Maastricht University Faculty of Law. The Maastricht Law Series publishes books on comparative, European and International law. The series builds upon the tradition of excellence in research at the Maastricht Faculty of Law, its research centers and the Ius Commune Research School. The Maastricht Law Series is a peer reviewed book series that allows researchers an excellent opportunity to showcase their work.

Published in this series:
Volume 1: Reinhard Zimmermann, Does the Law of Succession Reflect Cultural Differences?, ISBN 978-94-6236-856-9
Volume 2: Anna Berlee, Access to personal data in public land registers, ISBN 978-94-6236-841-5
Volume 3: Marcus Meyer, The Position of Dutch Works Councils in Multinational Corporations, ISBN 978-94-6236-848-4
Volume 4: Jaap Hage, Foundations and Building Blocks of Law, ISBN 978-94-6236-860-6
Volume 5: Bastiaan van Zelst, The End of Justice(s)?, ISBN 978-94-6236-881-1
Volume 6: Lars van Vliet & Agustin Parise (eds.), Re- De- Co-dification? New Insights on the Codification of Private Law, ISBN 978-94-6236-900-9
Volume 7: Caroline Rupp, Rafael Ibarra Garza & Bram Akkermans, Property Law Perspectives VI, ISBN 978-94-6236-904-7
Volume 8: Aalt Willem Heringa, Europees Nederlands Staatsrecht, ISBN 978-94-6290-604-4
Volume 9: Symeon C. Symeonides, The "Private" in Private International Law, ISBN 978-94-6236-949-8

Printed by Libri Plureos GmbH in Hamburg, Germany

9 789462 369498